Genre Fantasy

Essential Question
How can we work together to make our lives better?

MW00571693

Beware of the Lion!

by Vita Jiménez
illustrated by Dawn Beacon

CHAPTER 1

A Great Big Roar!

Deep in the grasslands of Africa lived a lion named Leopold. He roared when he was hungry. He roared when he was full. When he roared, animals from miles away could hear him.

When he roared, the grass in front of him would flatten, and the leaves would shake. His roar was that strong! All of the animals were afraid of him.

CHAPTER 2

A Very Hungry Lion

Leopold was a very hungry lion. He was so big that he needed to eat a lot in order to get full. He ate meat, leaves, fruit, and anything else he could find in the grasslands.

One day, a group of monkeys went out in search of food. They couldn't find much.

"Leopold has eaten most of our food!" said Max.

"What are we going to do?" asked Mavis. "We can't stop him. He's bigger and stronger than all of us."

Later that day, the zebras went out in search of food. They couldn't find much either.

"This is Leopold's fault! He's eating our grass and shrubs," said Zev.

"But what can we do? We're all afraid of him," said Zeena.

Later that same day, the giraffes were roaming the grasslands, trying to find some food.

"Leopold has done it again," said Gia. "He has eaten so many leaves that our children don't have enough to eat. But there are still some leaves on the branches at the very top."

"Those are hard to reach, even with our long necks," said George.

The monkeys heard the giraffes talking.

"If the giraffes are upset, then the problem is not just with us," said Max. "Leopold's hunger is hurting us all. Let's call an emergency meeting so that we can figure out an answer to this problem."

The monkeys spread the word, and a meeting was held that very night.

Some animals brought other animals. Everyone was there.

"We need to demand that Leopold stop eating our food," said Zeena.

"That's easy to say, but I'm afraid of him," said Mavis.

"We all are," said Max. "But let's talk to him together. Maybe all we need to do is open the door to a friendship."

"Let's try," said Gia. "I saw him earlier at the other watering hole."

CHAPTER 3

Friends Helping Friends

When they found Leopold, he was busy drinking water. He saw the animals and roared. But the animals kept coming. He roared again, but the animals kept coming. Leopold widened his eyes in surprise.

"Aren't you afraid of me?" said Leopold.

"Not anymore. We're afraid of something else," said Max. "We're afraid that if you don't stop, you will eat all our food."

"But I'm hungry," said Leopold.

"I know," said Zev. "But we're hungry, too. You have to share what's left, until more food grows."

"We'll show you how," said George. "We will tell you when we have extra food. You can't just come and take it. Friends don't do that."

"Are you all my friends?" asked Leopold.

"Yes," said Mavis. "And friends work together to help each other."

"I can do that," said Leopold. "I've never had so many friends!"

Respond to Reading

Retell

Use your own words to retell *Beware of the Lion!*

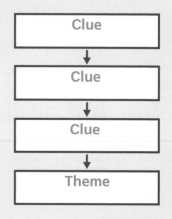

Text Evidence

1. How do the animals work together to help one another? Theme

2. What is the theme or message of this story? Theme

3. How do you know that *Beware of the Lion!* is a fantasy? Genre

Compare Texts

How do we help one another?

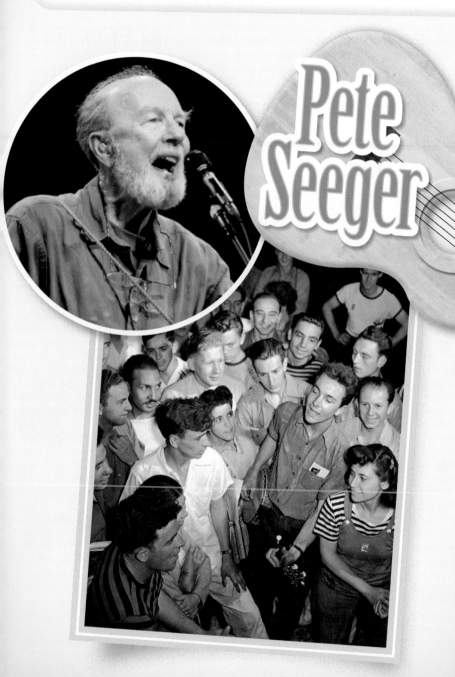

Pete Seeger

Pete Seeger was born in 1919. He is known around the world for the folk songs that he writes and sings.

A lot of his songs are about how people can work together to fix problems. One problem he sings about is pollution. He has taught people that it is important to clean up pollution in rivers.

People like to hear Pete Seeger sing.

Pete Seeger has helped people.

Pete Seeger also sings about the unfair ways people are treated. In the 1960s, he and many others tried to help African Americans get equal rights. Pete's songs made people aware of the problem.

Pete and his friends wrote new words to a song called "We Shall Overcome." When people want to fight unfairness together, they still sing this song.

Make Connections

Look at both selections. How can we come together to fix problems? Text to Text

Focus on
Genre

Fantasy Fantasy is a story that has made-up characters, settings, or other things that could not exist in real life.

What to Look for In *Beware of the Lion!* the animals talk to one another and find a way to solve a problem. Real animals don't do these things.

Your Turn

Pretend you're an animal who has a lot of food. You see another animal who doesn't have enough food to eat. Write a story about what you will do. Draw pictures to go with the story.